FINDING YOUR
Inner Goddess

A JOURNAL OF SELF-EMPOWERMENT

By Ama Patterson

Illustrated by Anne Smith

PETER PAUPER PRESS, INC.
White Plains, New York

Designed by Heather Zschock

Illustrations copyright © 2003 Anne Smith/Lilla Rogers Studio

Copyright © 2003
Peter Pauper Press, Inc.
202 Mamaroneck Avenue
White Plains, NY 10601
All rights reserved
ISBN 0-88088-270-0
Printed in Hong Kong
7 6 5 4 3 2 1

Visit us at www.peterpauper.com

Contents

Introduction 4

Great Goddesses 7

The Goddess Trinity 35

Nature's Rhythms 45

In Tune with Your Intuition 48

Worship Me 55

Worship Me #2..58

Worship Me #3..62

Goddess Journal 66

The Goddess Pledge......................................155

Which Goddess Are You? 156

Introduction

She is known by many names and wears many faces. She is the life cycle of this Earth: birth, death, renewal. She is the sensual blossoming of the Maiden, the fierce nurturing of the Mother, the wisdom of the Crone. She is the Egyptian Nut, who embodies the entire universe. She is the Sun, the Moon; she is fiery volcanoes and fathomless oceans. She is Mother of the First Dawn, the Creator of Life, and the Queen of Heaven. She is Strength, Love, Wisdom, Beauty, Knowledge, Honor, and Compassion. She is the Goddess, and she lives within every woman.

Ancient cultures the world over worshiped the Female Divine as the source of all life, from the bounty of the harvest to the miracle of childbirth. Small wonder women were the focus of a nature-based spirituality that valued family and community, and practiced harmony with the rhythms of the Earth. When we access the qualities of the Goddess and use them to enrich our daily lives, we are claiming our birthright.

There is that of the Goddess in every woman. Each of us is a unique and singular expression of the feminine Divine—a goddess in her own right. Your Inner Goddess is your highest, best, and most authentic Self.

Finding the Goddess Within requires both attention and action. We must pay mindful attention to the callings of our hearts and souls, and act in ways that enhance our highest selves. Honoring the Goddess Within means honoring our true selves. It means caring for our physical, emotional, and spiritual well-being so that our thoughts and actions come from a place of balance, where the Goddess resides.

This journal will help you connect with the many aspects of the Goddess within. Seek Her. Draw on Her strength, wisdom, creativity, and love to empower you in pursuit of your highest ideals. Celebrate yourself through all the stages of your life. The Goddess is you.

A. P.

Great Goddesses

AMATERASU •

Origin: Shinto/Japan
Symbol: The Sun
Qualities: radiance, warmth, abundance, healing, joy, benevolence

When Amaterasu became angry with her brother, she hid away in her cave, leaving heaven and earth in darkness. The goddesses and gods staged a bawdy revel at the mouth of her cave to draw her out. Once Amaterasu caught sight of her own dazzling reflection, she joyfully restored her light to the universe.

■ Are you hiding your light in a dusty cave? List three of your favorite interests or activities.

Here is where your skills and talents lie!

■ Now name three ways in which you can share your gifts with others.

AMATERASU'S MANTRA: I delight in my self; I shine and inspire.

• 8 •

ATHENA •

Origin: Greek

Qualities: war, strategy, handcrafts, wisdom, enlightenment

Although more famous for her dramatic birth (fully grown and armor-clad from the head of Zeus) and warrior's skills, Athena also presides over the peacetime employment of weavers, potters, and all endeavors requiring skill, planning, and execution. Astute, logical and hardworking, Athena is the consummate strategist. Education and professional achievement is her modern realm.

■ Describe the work you do now.

■ What (if anything) would you change?

■ Describe your ideal job in detail: work environment, schedule, tasks, and salary.

■ What steps will take you closer to achieving your dream?

ATHENA'S MANTRA: I plan my work and I work my plan.

Kuan Yin •

Origin: Buddhism/China
Other names: Great Mother of China, Goddess of Mercy,
"She Who Hearkens to the Cries of the World and Comes"
Qualities: compassion, sacrifice, healing

A Bodhisattva whose boundless compassion for all humanity inspires her to remain on Earth in human form until all living creatures attain Enlightenment, Kuan Yin is the epitome of kindness, empathy, and helpfulness. Her name refers not only to the Earth (Kuan), but to the universal feminine energy (Yin) that stands in eternal balance to the masculine (Yang).

■ "Do unto others as you would have others do unto you." The Golden Rule is the foundation of compassionate action. Describe an instance where you demonstrated compassion for another.

■ Describe an instance where you demonstrated compassion toward yourself.

KUAN YIN'S MANTRA: I treat myself and others with kindness and respect.

• 14 •

Ix Chel •

Origin: Maya/Mexico
Symbols: moon, water
Qualities: fertility, childbirth, health, healing

The Mayan "Lady Rainbow" pours life giving water down upon a thirsty earth. Women rely on her protection and comfort in childbirth. She is the Goddess of Medicine and patroness of traditional healers, who shows us the healing gifts of the Earth and the restorative powers of our own bodies. Her flower is the marigold and her totem is the snake, symbol of regeneration and rebirth.

■ Good health is not achieved by merely treating symptoms. Plan for yourself an appropriate diet, moderate exercise, relief from stress, and adequate rest to help your body find its natural balance.

List any habits or practices that stand between you and optimum health.

1.

2.

3.

4.

5.

6.

7.

8.

9.

10.

■ Select one and commit to changing it. Make a plan with a time frame. (Example: As of tonight I will no longer crunch potato chips while I watch the 11 o'clock news!)

Ix Chel's Mantra: I accept the Divine gift of good health.

KALI MA •

Origin: Hindu/India

Other name: The Destroyer

Attributes: time, eternity, life/death cycle, awareness, courage

When the Great Goddess Durga was attacked by the demon army, Kali Ma sprang from Durga's head, roaring and brandishing her sword, decapitating the advancing demons and drinking their blood. In full command of the cycle of life and death, Kali has an intensity that destroys evil, shatters obstacles, and clears the way for new growth.

◼ Do you have difficulty feeling or expressing anger?

■ What makes you angry?

■ Describe how it feels to acknowledge your anger.

_____

_____

_____

_____

_____

_____

_____

_____

_____

_____

_____

_____

_____

_____

_____

_____

_____

_____

_____

KALI MA'S MANTRA: As I acknowledge and express my anger, I reclaim my power.

HESTIA •

Origin: Greek

Qualities: family, household, and community; wholeness, centeredness

Of all twelve goddesses and gods in the Greek pantheon, first-born Hestia never took part in the wars or love affairs that characterized the fractious interactions of the others, preferring to maintain a constant presence as the sacred fire in the round hearth that made every home and temple sacred. Hestia is the center of the home and the family, gathering her loved ones around her.

■ Who is your family? Is it your parents, siblings, and other relatives who lovingly share your life? Or have you gathered around you a close network of true-blue friends?

■ Plan the ideal gathering for your family.

Guest list:

Location/date:

Food:

Activities:

HESTIA'S MANTRA: I am the constant fire around which my loved ones may gather.

• 23 •

■ Where is "home" for you? Is it the place of your childhood, wherever you rest your luggage, or is it some distant place you have yet to find? Describe "home"— where it is, what it looks like.

■ Who or what is there?

AFFIRMATION:
I am always at home in myself and in the world.
I am at home in the universe.

• 25 •

ISIS •

Origin: Kehmet/Egypt

Attributes: life, motherhood, nature, immortality, power, love

Speaking words of power, Isis resurrected her murdered husband Osiris, conceived a child with him, and granted him eternal life. She represents the magic within us: the sacred gift of our unique, individual spirits, and the limitless transformative power available to us when our spirits are attuned to the Divine.

■ What acts, practices, or rituals renew your spiritual connection?

Isis's Mantra: I embrace my inner Divinity.

CERRIDWEN •
Origin: Celtic/British Isles
Attributes: wisdom, knowledge, agriculture, death, transformation

Cerridwen sometimes appears as The White Sow, symbolizing death, and sometimes as a sage Crone. The Welsh poet Taliesin, composer of funeral elegies, claimed to have received his lyrical gifts straight from her boiling cauldron. Cerridwen distills knowledge and wisdom into inspiration.

■ Gaining wisdom takes time; it must be carefully brewed in the cauldron of learning and experience. What would you like to learn more about?

CERRIDWEN'S MANTRA: As I grow in experience, I grow in wisdom.

LAKSHMI •
Origin: Hindu/India
Qualities: wealth, prosperity

Lakshmi, Goddess of Wealth and Prosperity, is the power behind her consort Vishnu, The Preserver. She manifests in all forms of wealth, from coins and jewels to family and friends. Standing or seated on a lotus, she bears lotuses in her outstretched hands. Multiplicity and abundance are her gifts, and she is generous, indeed.

■ What is prosperity? Is it having lots of money, or does your definition go beyond material wealth?

LAKSHMI'S MANTRA: I have plenty of what I want and need in life.

ERZULIE •

Origin: Voudon/Haiti

Qualities: love, beauty, sensuality, fortune, creativity, water

Representative of human creativity and idealism, best known as a goddess of love and sensuality, Erzulie has a fondness for beauty and luxury. Always coiffed, powdered, perfumed, and fabulously attired, she loves dancing and receiving lavish gifts, especially flowers and jewels. As generous as she is alluring, Erzulie can also be vain, jealous, petty, or vengeful when she feels slighted or rejected. Erzulie reminds us that in order to love, we must first learn to love ourselves.

■ Have you ever experienced unconditional love? How did it feel?

■ Have you shown unconditional love to others? Write about this experience.

ERZULIE'S MANTRA: I love and accept myself as I am.

The Goddess Trinity

The Goddess often manifests as a trinity. The Three Fates of ancient Rome are one example: Clotho the Spinner creates the thread of mortal life, Lachesis the Measurer allots life's length, and Atropos the Cutter determines its end. The Zorya of Slavic tradition—She of the Evening, She of Midnight, and She of Morning—are another. One more triune manifestation is the Virgin, the Mother, and the Crone. As such, the Goddess embodies the passages of mortal life: birth, growth, and death. These stages correspond to the cycles of the Earth—creation, preservation, and destruction; the seasonal transitions from spring to summer to winter; and the moon waxing, full, and waning.

■ The Virgin is birth and possibility: springtime, new life, and new ventures. In what area(s) of your life are you a Maiden? New career? New relationship? Your first child or your first snowboarding lesson? In each case, you are an initiate. How does it feel to be at the beginning?

■ The Mother nurtures, sustains, and defends that which you have brought into being. Think summer—your creation is ripe, ready to be savored. What fills you with a sense of satisfaction and accomplishment?

■ The Crone: old, decrepit, and useless? Not so! The Crone is the wisdom and humor of experience. She stirs her bubbling cauldron of knowledge gained through trial and triumph. Like harvested grain, she is the seed of future possibilities. In what areas of life have you gained Crone wisdom?

■ How can you best share your Crone knowledge with others?

Nature's Rhythms

Days, seasons, tides, and phases of the moon are all the province of the Goddess. Her energy flows with the rhythmic cycles of nature. Too often, our lives leave little time to appreciate nature's rhythms, or our own.

■ Make time to watch a sunrise or sunset. Observe the shifts of light and color; be aware of sounds around you. Or: go to the beach. Sit where you can see the waves and hear them splash upon the sand. Jot down whatever thoughts occur. Go with the flow.

In Tune with Your Intuition

Intuition is the voice of the Goddess speaking truth to our hearts. It's that gut feeling or sudden knowing that comes from beyond our physical senses. Our intuition makes us aware of hidden possibilities and implications, and empowers us to live confidently and make sound decisions.

We must accustom ourselves to heeding that inner Voice. Intuition is like a muscle—it grows stronger with use.

■ Often our intuition speaks through a knot in the gut, a sudden rush of energy, or a twinge of anxiety. Practice paying attention to your physical senses. Take five or ten minutes to focus on what each of your senses is telling you right now before writing the responses.

Sight:

Sound:

Smell:

Taste:

Touch:

■ What/how does your body feel right now? Are you comfortable?
Why or why not?

_____

_____

_____

_____

_____

_____

_____

■ Identify your present feelings and emotions. Don't judge yourself for having
them, or feel that you have to do anything about them; just name them.

I feel _____

_____

_____

_____

_____

_____

_____

_____

_____

■ Our thoughts allow us to understand our emotions and put them into perspective. Can you determine why you feel what you noted above? Think about whether your feelings and reason enhance and empower you or drain and limit you. You may decide you are ready to "move on" from some patterns of feeling. For example, you might decide you are ready to discard feeling shy about public speaking because as a child you were teased about your lisp.

I feel _____

because _____

_____

_____

_____

_____

_____

_____

_____

_____

_____

_____

■ Recall a time when you followed your intuition in making a decision, rather than your reason. Describe the situation and the result.

■ Meditation: Open yourself to the presence of the Divine. Imagine sacred Energy surrounding and flowing through your body.

The Top Ten

■ Whether their names are on banners and billboards worldwide or simply legendary in your neighborhood, these women strive to be the best they can be, and inspire you to do the same. List your top ten personal Goddesses.

1. _____ , because

_____

_____

2. _____ , because

_____

_____

3. _____ , because

_____

_____

4. _____ , because

_____

_____

5. _____ , because

_____

6. _____ , because _____

_____

_____

7. _____ , because _____

_____

_____

8. _____ , because _____

_____

_____

9. _____ , because _____

_____

_____

10. _____ , because _____

_____

_____

_____

Worship Me

Lose the humility and modesty for the moment. Brag. Beat your own drum. What do you love about yourself? What do you excel at? List your natural talents, skills, accomplishments, and adventures—the many reasons why you rock!

Note: Refer to this list on days when you are feeling less than Goddess-like!

Worship Me #2

Back when the world was new, everything here was dark, yet people on the other side of the world had plenty of light from the sun. Other animals tried and failed to bring the sun to this side of the world—it was too hot for them to carry. Then Grandmother Spider, Kanene Ski Amai Yehi, spoke up, saying, "I will bring the sun." She made a great basket, and spun a web to take her all the way to the other side of the world. No one noticed the tiny spider creeping determinedly along a gossamer strand of web. When she reached the other side of the world, she waited until no one was looking, then popped the sun into her basket and crept quickly back the way she came. The people rejoiced at her return, for Grandmother Spider brought the gift of light.
—Cherokee/North America

YOUR MYTH HERE

■ What's your myth? Your tale of daring, heroism, righteous retaliation or noble sacrifice? Be as factual or as whimsical as you wish—this is the legend of you.

Worship Me #3

POSTHUMOUS DEIFICATION— IT COULD HAPPEN TO YOU!

Nefertari, Goddess of Justice, was once a mortal queen who ruled Egypt from 1546 to 1526 B.C.E. Indonesian Rain Goddesses Trung Trac and her sister Trung Nhi were originally warrior women who led a successful revolt against a foreign tyrant. So, hey . . . it could happen!

■ What's your name? What kind of Goddess will you be? What's your temple like? Describe the rituals and offerings that please you. Any holidays in your honor? Do it up! After all, you're a Goddess!

_____

_____

_____

_____

_____

_____

_____

_____

_____

_____

_____

_____

_____

_____

Goddess Journal

These pages are for logging

your journey to the INNER YOU.

Tell me, what is it you plan to do with your one wild and precious life?
MARY OLIVER

People who succeed speak well of themselves to themselves.

LAURIE BETH JONES

*You have control over three things—what you think, what you say and how
you behave. To make a change in your life, you must recognize that these gifts
are the most powerful tools you possess in shaping the form of your life.*

SONYA FRIEDMAN

Don't be too choosy or stingy about whom or how often you love.
HELEN GURLEY BROWN

Learning to embrace and dance with change allows you
to create a life of accomplishment and exhilaration.

CANDICE CARPENTER

I am in the world to change the world.

MURIEL RUKEYSER

Being loved anyway is not being regarded
as perfect but being accepted as imperfect.

ELLEN GOODMAN

Everyone has talent. What is rare is the courage to follow the talent to the dark place where it leads.

ERICA JONG

You don't just luck into things. . . . You build step by step,
whether it's friendships or opportunities.

BARBARA BUSH

In my apron, I carry nails, pliers, a heavy hammer, and pride.
MOIRA BACHMAN

Stick to three concepts. You can't help everyone.
You can't change everything. Not everyone is going to love you.
ROBERTA VASKO KRAUS

Too many women in too many countries
speak the same language—silence.
ANASUYA SENGUPTA

We must learn and reach from a source of creativity—that wellspring of expression—
because once we drink of those waters, our vision changes and we become free.

Phylicia Rashad

Confidence is based on the ability you have,
not what somebody else has.

JOAN MONDALE

So many people walk around without knowing who they are and what
they are and want to be. As long as you are searching, you are on the path.
Dare yourself to step on the path. Be brave and take that step.

KIM COLES

Love me in full being.

ELIZABETH BARRETT BROWNING

Every single day, we can make our lives brand new.
We can be the best we can be. . . . Know that if you lift yourself
up and dust yourself off, you'll find a better you underneath.

EMME

The Goddess Pledge

I,_____,

do hereby affirm that

I Am a Goddess.

The power of the

Feminine Divine is Within Me.

I claim my beauty and my strength,

my dignity and humor,

my passion and compassion.

I honor myself as I honor all life.

Which Goddess Are You?

Choose your response to each situation and
discover your true Goddess nature!

■ You work for a mid-size company. A position in another department one level above yours has become available. Your company is doing outside hiring. You want that job!

You:

1. Grumble and fume to your friends at lunch about the unfairness of the situation.
2. Carefully compose a letter detailing your rightness for the position, and send it to the boss with a request for an interview.
3. Tell your supervisor over lunch that you feel ready for additional responsibility. Casually mention the open position.
4. Start updating your resume and contacts list. If the company is looking elsewhere, then so will you.

Answers:

1. Kali Ma: Constructive expression of anger or frustration is healthy. Sometimes it's necessary to vent with trusted friends—but don't let that be a substitute for action.
2. Athena: A well-planned, bold move!
3. Spider Grandmother: Cunning and stealth. Weave your web carefully to get the prize.
4. Cerridwen: Sometimes you just have to know when to cut your losses and move on.

■ You're casually browsing in your favorite boutique and see the most beautiful ring—hand crafted, one of a kind. It fits perfectly and looks great, but truthfully it's more than you can afford.

You:

1. Put the ring on layaway. Ten percent down, and it will be on your finger by next month.
2. Charge! Your credit balance is already so high, what's the difference? You want it now!
3. Grit your teeth, review your long term financial goals, and leave the ring on the counter.
4. Review your list of people who might be motivated to give you a gift . . . just because.

Answers:

1. Lakshmi: See? You can have what you want and what you need. There is plenty!
2. Kali Ma: Yes, NOW, but beware! Ravenous needs have their consequences!
3. Athena: That's right, stick with your plan—that's worth much more than a ring!
4. Erzulie: For . . . me? Why, thank you!

■ You come home from work exhausted, to a disaster of used dishes, laundry, and displaced items. Oblivious to the chaos, your loved ones sit watching television, and greet you with: "Hi. What's for dinner?"

You:

1. Reply: "Whatever you're cooking, dear," and head straight for a bubble-bath.
2. Rip the TV cable out of its box, and blast your dear ones for their sloth and selfishness.
3. Hurriedly swap your suit for sweats, and begin your second shift.
4. State loudly and clearly: "I've had a hard day, and I need you to clean up and fix dinner."

Answers:

1. Ix Chel: That's right, dear. Sometimes the caretaker needs care! Take a break. Run the water. Ahhhh . . .
2. Kali Ma: Let 'em have it! How DARE they treat me this way!
3. Hestia: Yes, I know you enjoy creating a cozy home, but just be sure they're not using you for the doormat!
4. Cerridwen: Firm, but patient—a sign of wisdom. Just let them know they can stir the cauldron themselves tonight!

■ You, your best friend, and her neighbor have been enjoying occasional coffee dates and nights out until they have an argument—the kind where neither of them is on the right side of the issue.

You:
1. Contact the feuding factions and recommend meeting for peace talks—you'll buy the coffee!
2. Continue to enjoy time with each friend separately.
3. Tell the neighbor that any enemy of your best friend is no friend of yours . . . or something like that!
4. Make yourself scarce until they both start acting like the friends you knew.

1. Kuan Yin: Helping them heal the rift is a true act of compassion.
2. Amaterasu: Why should you deprive yourself of the pleasure of each friend's company? Let them know how you feel, and trust that they will reconcile in time.
3. Hestia: Loyalty to friends is a gift, but it needn't be harshly expressed.
4. Erzulie: Isn't it time for my six-month holiday?

■ Your five-year-old comes running to you on the playground. Other kids are hogging the swings!

You:
1. Sweep down on the offenders and scare them into sharing.
2. Look around for the parents of the little brats.
3. Tell your child to go tell the other kids that she wants a turn, too.
4. Gently suggest that she play with something else for now.

Answers:
1. Kali Ma: No offense (or offender) is too small for retribution!
2. Athena: This is one task I can delegate!
3. Hestia: A just, balanced, and highly instructive response!
4. Kuan Yin: A little peace . . . for the moment!